Penguin Day

A FAMILY STORY

BY **Nic Bishop**

SCHOLASTIC PRESS | NEW YORK

Morning has come and baby penguin is hungry. Baby penguin is too little to get breakfast, so mama penguin will go hunting.

Papa penguin will stay behind to keep an eye on the little one.

Mama penguin has a big journey ahead of her. She and the other penguins will travel far to get food for their families.

They will scamper over hills . . .

. . . and climb down cliffs.

They will hop across sand . . .

. . . until finally
they reach the sea.

The sea is dangerous
and filled with
predators like orcas
and sea lions. The
penguins are
nervous.

There is safety in numbers, so mama and the other penguins all jump in at once!

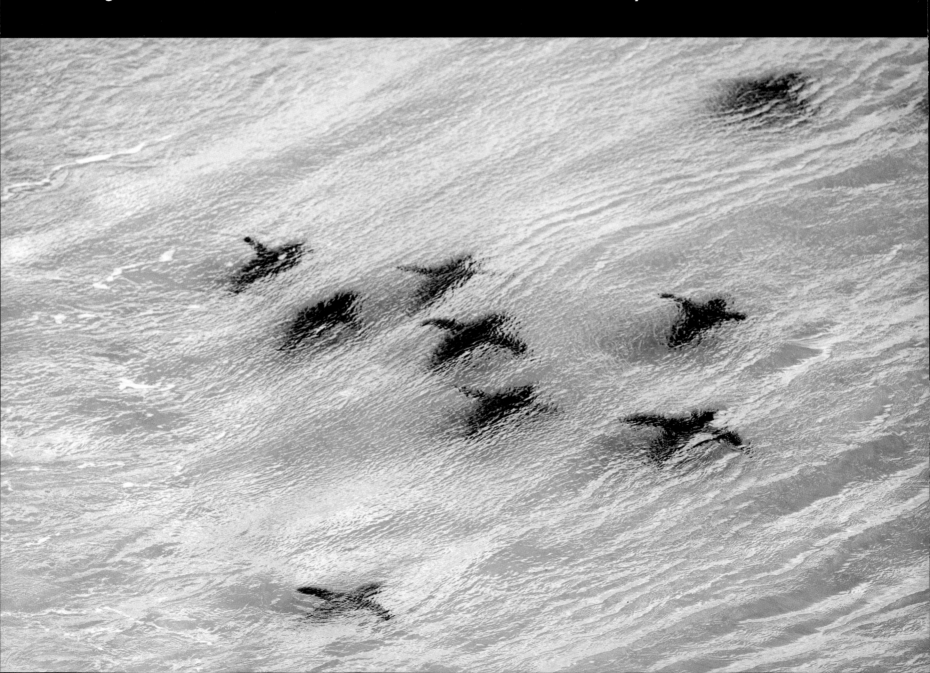

hunting for fish and krill.

Meanwhile, back at home, baby penguin is getting hungrier and hungrier and really wants to eat!

Baby penguin wanders off to visit some friends.

But they are too sleepy to play.

So baby penguin

waddles away alone.

Far away, mama penguin is filling her belly with fish and krill. Soon she'll be on her way home to feed her baby.

The penguins leap from the sea.

. . . and start the journey home.

While walking, baby penguin sees something in the sky.

It's a skua, and she is just as hungry as baby penguin.

The skua swoops down on baby penguin.

But papa penguin saves the day! He frightens off the skua. Now baby penguin is safe.

Papa penguin and baby penguin head back to the colony . . .

. . . where mama penguin is waiting with food. Now baby penguin can eat.

Papa penguin is happy to see mama penguin, too.

It has been a long day, and baby penguin is tired.

Sleep tight,

baby penguin.

Author's Note

The penguins in this book are called southern rockhopper penguins. They live in the cold, southern oceans that surround Antarctica.

In spring, the penguins breed on remote, rocky islands. They nest on the ground in large, noisy colonies that can have thousands of birds. The parents take turns looking after the eggs. But when the chicks hatch, the male stays behind to guard the young while the female goes to sea to catch krill, fish, and squid.

Southern rockhoppers are one of the smallest types of penguins. They only stand about twenty inches tall, but they are tough. As the female dives for food, she has to dodge predators such as orcas, sharks, and sea lions. She also has to swim through some of the stormiest seas on earth. When she returns to her colony, she often has to climb steep cliffs rising more than a hundred feet from the sea.

A southern rockhopper penguin

Penguins battling huge waves

Penguin stopping for a wash

As they climb, the penguins may stop for a wash in freshwater streams or waterfalls. They like to clean the salt and mud from their feathers. When a female finally reaches her family there is lots of excited calling as everyone recognizes each other. Then the mother regurgitates the food she swallowed at sea into the mouth of her hungry chick.

Life can be dangerous for the chicks. They have to deal with predators, too, especially skuas. Skuas need to find food for their own young, and they are quick to grab any penguin egg or young chick left unguarded by a parent.

As a penguin chick gets older, it becomes more curious about its surroundings. But it can get into trouble if it strays from its parents. By the time it is three or four weeks old, the chick will join a group of other chicks, called a crèche. Being in a crèche helps keep the chick safe from predators, so both its parents can go to sea to catch food. The parents continue to feed the chick, and by the time it is about ten weeks old it will lose its soft, downy coat for a sleek covering of waterproof feathers. Soon it is ready to head out to sea.

A skua chick

A Note About the Photographs

The author spent three weeks photographing rockhopper penguins for this book. Severe gales and freezing temperatures often made things difficult for him but never daunted the penguins. Every day they ventured into stormy seas and climbed home over tall cliffs, meeting each challenge with feisty determination. More than one chick and its parents were photographed to make this book. To learn more about the photographs, visit www.nicbishop.com.

Library of Congress Cataloging-in-Publication Data
Names: Bishop, Nic, 1955– author, illustrator.
Title: Penguin day : a family story / by Nic Bishop.
Description: First edition. | New York : Scholastic Press, 2017.
Identifiers: LCCN 2016024913 | ISBN 9780545206365 (hc)
Subjects: LCSH: Eudyptes chrysocome — Juvenile literature. | Penguins — Infancy — Juvenile literature.
Classification: LCC QL696.S473 B57 2017 | DDC 598.47 — dc23
LC record available at https://lccn.loc.gov/2016024913

10 9 8 7 6 5 4 3 2 1   17 18 19 20 21

Printed in Malaysia   108
First edition, March 2017

The text type was set in Abadi MT Condensed Regular.
Book design by Marijka Kostiw